THE SHORT-FICTION SCENARIO

EISEN

SERGEI

STEIN

The Short-Fiction
Scenario

TRANSLATED BY *Alan Upchurch*

LONDON NEW YORK CALCUTTA

SEAGULL BOOKS, 2017

First published by Seagull Books in 1984

English translation © Seagull Books, 1984

ISBN 978 0 85742 489 1

British Library Cataloguing-in-Publication Data
A catalogue record for this book is available from the British Library

Typeset by Manasij Dutta, Seagull Books, Calcutta, India
Printed and bound in the United States by Maple Press, York, PA
Printed and bound in India by WordsWorth India, New Delhi

LIST OF ABBREVIATIONS

In the notes, Sergei Eisenstein is referred to as E and the following abbreviations are used for the commonly cited works:

ESW1: Sergei Eisenstein, *Selected Works, Volume 1*: *Writings, 1922–34* (Richard Taylor ed. and trans.). London: BFI, 1988.

ESW2: Sergei Eisenstein, *Selected Works, Volume 2*: *Towards a Theory of Montage* (Michael Glenny ed., R. Taylor trans.). London: BFI, 1991.

ESW3: Sergei Eisenstein, *Selected Works, Volume 3*: *Writings, 1934–47* (Richard Taylor ed., William Powell trans.). London: BFI, 1996.

ESW4: Sergei Eisenstein, *Beyond the Stars: The Memoirs of Sergei Eisenstein* (Richard Taylor ed., William Powell trans.). Calcutta: Seagull Books, 1995.

ER: Richard Taylor (ed.), *The Eisenstein Reader* (Richard Taylor and William Powell trans). London: BFI, 1998.

ERD: Ian Christie and Richard Taylor (eds), *Eisenstein Rediscovered*. London: Routledge, 1993.

FF: Richard Taylor and Ian Christie (eds), *The Film Factory: Russian and Soviet Cinema in Documents, 1896–1939* (Richard Taylor trans.). London: Routledge & Kegan Paul, 1988.

FEL: Sergei Eisenstein, *Film Essays and a Lecture* (Jay Leyda ed. and trans.). Princeton, NJ: Princeton University Press, 1982.

FiFo: Sergei Eisenstein, *Film Form: Essays in Film Theory*, (Jay Leyda ed. and trans.). New York: Harcourt, Brace Jovanovich, 1949.

FS: Sergei Eisenstein, *The Film Sense* (Jay Leyda ed. and trans.). New York: Harcourt, Brace Jovanovich, 1942.

IP: *Izbrannye proizvedeniia v shesti tomakh* [Selected Works in Six Volumes] (S. I. Iutkevich et al. eds). Moscow: Iskusstvo, 1964–71.

NIN: Sergei Eisenstein, *Nonindifferent Nature: Film and the Structure of Things* (Herbert Marshall ed. and trans.). Cambridge: Cambridge University Press, 1987.

RGALI: Rossiiskii gosudarstvennyi arkhiv literatury i iskusstv [Russian State Archive for Literature and the Arts], Moscow.

VGIK: Vsesoiuznyi gosudarstvennyi institut kinmetaografii [All-Union State Cinema Institute], Moscow.

THE SHORT-FICTION SCENARIO[1]

The war facing Soviet cinema has given rise to a specific task: the creation of a short-film repertoire—something we have not had previously.

For a long time now many people, including myself, have insisted that we should begin producing short films. I suggested to the script studio that an experimental group be formed to analyse the composition of the short fictional film. My suggestion did not receive enough support and the matter was dropped.

You will recall Lenin's famous film proportion programme, which called for a number of different formats—dramatic, newsreel, etc.[2] There is now an attempt being made in the film albums [*boevye kinosborniki*] to fulfil this Leninist proportion, but not on a high enough level. The quality of this production is inferior to the achievements of directors and scriptwriters working in the full-length format. Why is this? These people cannot be blamed for a lack of enthusiasm or patriotism. It is because there has been no experience in constructing the short fictional film. No one has dealt with it in either theory or practice. And, when the time came to make these films quickly, efficiently and at first, under difficult conditions, we found ourselves unprepared.

Directors of the highest calibre are coping better with the task. Pudovkin's *Feast at Zhirmunka*[3] will be a fine picture, no less than his other films. True, it will exceed the traditional length of a short fictional film; it will run to 1,000 to 2,000 metres, whereas the standard length of the short film is 500 to 600 metres. But any creative attempt is interesting and helpful to us. Later, I will read out to you two versions of this script where the same situation is developed—superficially in one case, but in the second, (written by a true writer, Leonid Leonov)[4] at a quite different level.

In the context of the composition of the short film, I shall talk about montage. This should not surprise you. Those who have read my writings from 1935, in particular my speech at the Cinema Conference,[5] should pay attention to a particular point that I made: that montage is essentially micro-dramaturgy.

This means:

that the meaning and peculiarities of montage comprise the most minute and condensed dramaturgical solutions,

that the principle of composition, of combining three or four pieces in a montage phrase, is the same as the joining of three scenes within an act (or five acts) in a play,

and that through montage we can trace the same laws which are repeated (with qualitative adjustments) in the compositional structure of the full-length and even serial film.

In the past few years, so-called montage cinema has gone out of style. Seven or eight years ago, it was still in great favour. But then a number of people (basically those who do not know how to edit) proclaimed a 'liberation from the shackles of montage'.[6] What this led to is evidenced by a deficit of several million roubles at Mosfilm. The replacement of montage by the long take makes impossible something as simple as tightening up poorly paced shots. If this happens at the end of a film, where five thousand horsemen are shot from an aircraft in long shot with no medium or close shots, then the tension is lost; this kind of mass scene [*massovka*] will produce no impression of any kind.

But this is not the greatest loss. Those who discarded montage have forgotten that it is, above all, an active method of narrative, that the exposition of an event through montage enables the viewer's attention to be captured and led along the necessary sequence of vision. Shooting in long take is almost always neutral and passive.

Let us say that you need to show a corpse lying in a room. If you present this in a single long take, then the viewer will begin looking at what took place. You permit him, as in life, to select details himself and focus his attention on what *he* wants, not what *you* want to show.

Before the war, a scene of a corpse being discovered would have been shot this way:

The scene would begin with a boot lying in the corner of the room.

Then we would be shown a ticking clock.

A window with curtains drawn.

An arm hanging over the side of the bed.

And only then—a man lying on the bed with his head smashed in.

In a traditional outline of this sort, the viewer follows each successive piece with new interest. Why is there a boot in the corner? Is he asleep? Or did he just come home and take it off? Your interest is heightened: what will happen next is unknown. You start to think: if it is night, then there is nothing unusual about a boot lying in a corner. But if it is day? The editor-director gives the first answer—the clock. The hands indicate 3.00. Another question: a.m. or p.m.? It has not yet been made clear. A shot of the window, daylight coming through the curtains. Something is wrong. An arm hangs over the side of the bed. Is he asleep? If it is a sound film, then the viewer can tell by listening. No breathing is heard, but something is dripping. (A silent film would show the blood dripping in close up.) And finally, you see that the man lying on the bed has been murdered.

And, so at each close shot, a turn occurs, a movement. But it is not known in which direction the action is headed. It does not progress as at first as you would want it to, but rather twists off in another direction. When everything develops straightforwardly, in a straight direct line, you are bored. The least correct approach to narrative is that which seems natural.

From the five shots in this trite example, one can recognize the outline which underlies the most complex subjects. What type of literature is structured according to this outline?

The detective novel. It is there that this method achieves a level of purity. The detective novel is the most riveting form of literature: you truly cannot tear yourself away from it.

In the detective novel, the composition, the choice of characters and the development of their personalities (with the triggering of unconditioned and conditioned reflexes), are all used in such a witty, simple and concrete manner, that the detective novel approaches classical literature. Detective novels such as those by Dostoyevsky (*The Brothers Karamazov* or *Crime and Punishment*)[7] combine a simple compositional development with the highest literary qualities. But, even without them, the detective novel makes a strong impact. It is unique because it makes, literally *makes*, its subject interesting.

How is the detective novel usually structured? By a gradual accumulation of evidence. The entire structure of Maurice Leblanc's story 'The Red Silk Scarf' hinges on Arsène Lupin and detectives hunting down a criminal.[8] Through various clues, Lupin is able to determine that the criminal wears a monocle, an overcoat with a fur collar and carries a heavy cane. Then he discovers what kind of hat the criminal wears. From these individual features a portrait emerges, but it remains sketchy until the end. The final detail: Lupin warns the Chief Inspector not to approach this man from his left side. The Chief Inspector, of course, ignores this warning and nearly gets shot, since the criminal is left-handed.

The other common outline of a detective novel is the shifting of suspicion. In this type of novel there are five to seven people, all equally capable of having committed the crime. But only one of them is really the criminal. The novel is structured in such a way that one chapter presents evidence of one person's guilt, a second chapter of another's, a third of the next one's, and so on. And, even though you know this formula, you cannot help but be caught up in the game.

I strongly urge you not to dismiss this genre of literature. Besides being quite entertaining, it can be of great investigative value to you. Once you start to analyse what takes place and how, you will begin comparing how it is done in different circumstances and genres. You will see that essentially, all the secrets of composition are contained within the detective novel. Even the fact that in every detective novel there is a death or murder is an example of using a situation that makes the strongest physiological impact.

What is most striking in the detective novel can also be found in more subtle form in other genres. Think of *Eugene Onegin*[9] or any novel by one of the masters. The character's personality gradually becomes clear to you as you read. In one scene, you sense the character's cruelty but in another, you see that all the same he possesses certain warm, human traits. In a third scene, he appeals to you but in a fourth it becomes clear that this scoundrel and his appeal are all pretence. And so, the man's image is drawn gradually. If a character is fully described on the first page and proceeds throughout the entire work like a mechanical doll, then the reader's interest is accordingly weakened.

Remember these lines from Pushkin:

Resplendent, half ethereal,
Obedient to the magic bow,
Surrounded by a throng of nymphs,
Istomina stands: she,[10]

Each 'shot' is a means of concealing Istomina before fully presenting her. Pushkin builds up the interest in her appearance.

To impress the viewer, to rivet his attention—we followed the same principle in constructing our five-shot montage sequence.

In the early period of montage cinema, our filmmakers shot such ordinary things as factory production effectively and with meaning. In Vertov's early work or the industrial films Tisse once shot, molten metal or some machine would be 'presented' in such an interesting and poetic manner, they would appear quite gripping.[11] Today, we have truly astonishing real-life material being shot, but inept editing. But this also applies to the shooting because montage is inseparable from the shooting process. The fall of montage inevitably entailed the impoverishment of montage thought at the shooting stage. It is often impossible to edit newsreel material because it has not been planned for in terms of montage.

What I am now talking about is directly related to the art of narrative construction. Unfortunately, our middle generation of filmmakers has almost completely lost this ability to construct a narrative in an interesting fashion.

In 1935, a group of directors, opposed to montage, praised certain American pictures many of which (films with Gary Cooper, for example) presented nothing special in terms of montage.[12] The succession of shots, the collision of shots, etc. played no role in their montage. This group did not realize that the secrets of what made these films interesting were concealed in the dramaturgical structuring of the dialogue. If you follow the dialogue of a traditional American sequence, you will see that in one episode there occurs such a forceful build-up of tension, acceleration of tempo and unexpected change in meaning, that even montage cannot keep up with it.

A straightforwardly developing narrative does not have to result in a boring work with a depressing succession of events. It can make for an exceptionally forceful action or dialogue, where each successive phrase elicits stronger interest and tension. This is how Ben Jonson structures his works.[13] The basic plot of his comedy, *Volpone*, involves a man who pretends to be rich even though he is completely in debt. He lives off his relatives, who are all older than him. At first, he borrows money from them, then their dishes and other possessions. And finally, so that he will not be bored, one old man lends Volpone his own wife.

My own films are usually built on a progressive accumulation of tension.

VOICE FROM THE ROOM: Doesn't that lead away from genre?

—It leads to genre.

Though it would seem simple, it is more difficult to make a linear compositional development interesting than a plot development. It is accomplished by attention to microscopic details, montage, rhythm, etc.

But we were saying that the principles of constructing a gripping plot and the principles of montage construction are identical.

The compositional methods of the detective novel are only particular cases of more general principles of the organization of material in a work. These same principles are used in dramaturgy, montage, plastic construction etc. We can generally formulate one of them in terms of the principle of *the breaking of inertia.*

First, a very simple example. Let us say that you make a movement as though about to strike someone. This will attract the attention of the person looking at you. But his impression will be much stronger if you then suddenly draw your hand back in the opposite direction and strike from there. The sudden change in direction breaks the inertia of the expected movement and therefore, creates a stronger impression.

This principle is related to man's ability to mentally *reconstruct a whole from a part*: a figure, a movement, a personality. Every person possesses this ability, but it must be especially developed in an artist. A true master can create the impression of a living character, not by describing the entire person in detail, but by merely presenting two or three traits (but precisely those traits by which the majority of people sense the whole).

Perhaps you are familiar with Lev Tolstoy's use of the 'passport' detail.[14] The characters in *War and Peace* bear certain details with them throughout the novel, say a swollen lip with a thin moustache. This same manner is easily recognized in Lion Feuchtwanger's works, but he uses it more crudely.[15] In *Jew Süss*, the margravine's snake-like, trembling neck is prominent throughout the entire book. With Tolstoy, this is handled subtly and less persistently.

Among the materials published by the Tolstoy Museum is a study by Evelina Zaidenshnur on the twelve variations of details used to help form the image of Katyusha Maslova.[16] Zaidenshnur compiled some very interesting charts through which it is possible to trace how many and which features Tolstoy considered necessary to ascribe to Katyusha's face at various stages of work. True, she did not attempt what would be of most interest to us here—a composite chart. As it turned out, three details were sufficient to impress Katyusha Maslova's appearance into our memory.

During your entrance exams, I demonstrated this ability to construct the whole from a part [*pars pro toto*] using this same number. We set up three chairs with galoshes in various positions underneath. One pair of galoshes with socks inside, another pair of galoshes with socks outside, and a single galosh. Based on the position of the galoshes, you had to describe what the characters sitting in the chairs looked like. Many were puzzled by the single galosh. Fifty per cent of the applicants inferred that it was a cripple.

This ability is also the basis of the phenomenon of movement in cinema. Frame after frame of immobile images follow each other in succession. From the first static image, you imagine a certain movement, and the following frame serves as a stimulus to the next phase. Optically, you can perceive an uninterrupted movement.

Now let us recall Daumier's drawings.[17] They belong to the most dynamic and lively examples of world art. Daumier's 'trick' is very simple. In drawing the figure of a man, he depicts the position of the feet so perfectly that the entire figure's movement is clearly imagined. You mentally construct the figure expected from these feet (this is done subconsciously), but Daumier shows you the central portion of the body, from the knees to the shoulders in a different phase of movement, and the position of the head is given in yet a third phase. As a result, you have the impression that the figure moved, jerked from phase to phase—as in cinema. This is aided by the choppy, sketchy quality of Daumier's drawings, which at times deform the physical shape of the body to the point that it appears as though the joint is broken off.

This same principle of interrupting the inertia of perception is used by Tintoretto,[18] but with more restraint than Daumier, with a less severe deformation of the body. His flying figures are literally depicted as a spiral.

Michelangelo does the same thing in sculpture.[19] Look at his tomb for the Medici. Each element of the body in the two reclining figures is in a different position of movement. But Michelangelo obtains a different effect through this. Daumier, by successively dismembering a figure, conveys a movement of the body. But with Michelangelo, although all the joints of the bodies *are* in different stages of movement, the figures are organized so as *not to give* a feeling of movement. In a certain way, he even tries *to bind* movement. This is intricately related to a psychological situation characteristic of Michelangelo's works. In spite of the awesome power of his works, they are all tragically constrained. And this feeling of tragic constraint (movement which strains, but cannot break loose) finds a plastic embodiment. Everything boils within, everything wants to burst forward, but is doomed to utter hopelessness. This principle of the destruction of movement is thematically very fitting for tomb statues and is wonderfully expressed in plastic.

Thus, the way in which the inertia of perception is interrupted determines the sensation being perceived. It is possible to obtain a sensation of straightforward, frontal, movement: movement with unexpected turns and jumps, self-balancing movement. And is not literary composition, in fact, marked by this same principle?

Before we analyse several novellas, I want to turn your attention to one more principal similarity between the montage process and prose writing.

In the past, we have discussed the concept of changing shooting angles for each new shot: a new shot is essentially a phenomenon viewed from a new position.

Now, let us recall the various ways of structuring a story.

A narrative can be conducted by an unidentified person throughout the whole novel. This can be either a neutral, objective account of events from the author's point of view, or by some narrator who does not participate in the events. For example, a border guard who relates the various events he witnesses from his point of view and with his commentary.

In some cases, this is taken further where a character recounts the events. Dr Watson, for example, talks about Sherlock Holmes and also participates in the events.[20]

There is also a type of literary work where the events are recounted from the points of view of several characters—from one character's in chapter one, from another's in chapter two and so on. There occurs a *change in the point of view towards the events being recounted.*

A very interesting example of this approach is the American poet Edgar Lee Masters' collection, *Spoon River*

Anthology.[21] He uses a terrific device. The author wanted to convey an image of a small American town with many characters and extremely complex, interlacing events. He creates a collection of poems in the form of epitaphs in the town's cemetery. Each epitaph is written as a monologue spoken by the deceased person. The author goes through the cemetery, making very curious comments about certain of the epitaphs. A piece of information about one body calls forth information about other bodies. A large, complex, interwoven pattern of relationships existing in this town is obtained, and it gradually unfolds by reading the epitaphs. For example, in one epitaph you learn of a fallen girl who was subjected to persecution. And lying next to her is the rich banker who ruined this girl. The funniest epitaph is on the headstone of a Puritan minister: 'Here I lie. All my life I struggled for the morality of our town. Why is it that the young nightly make my grave their unholy pillow?'

Joseph Conrad's co-author, Ford Madox Ford, describes in his memoirs how they set themselves the task of finding an indirect account of events, so boring had the English Victorian novel with its successive plot-unfolding become.[22] Where was the model found for the approach needed? One is reminded of the structure of E. T. A. Hoffmann's *The Life and Opinions of the Tomcat Murr*, where the pages seem scattered and arranged at random, as though several stories had been mixed up.[23] But Ford Madox Ford points to a true source of composition—life. Because in life, there is no logically successive order for the learning of events.

Let's say, you are playing golf and your partner strikes you as a fat, typically English gentleman, stable and composed. Soon, you learn that in his youth, this man had committed a forgery. Then you find out that he had donated a large sum to the needy. But two years later, he was convicted of bigamy.

This can be told not only from different characters' points of view, but with the help of a complex temporal composition. At first, the novel presents a man playing a game of golf. Then the action shifts to ten years earlier when you learn of the forgery. Next, here is the event which portrays him as kind-hearted and continues in this manner.

At present, cinema uses this kind of composition with less freedom than literature. Memories are usually presented in cinema via a dissolve. There is a more intelligent way, whereby a reference to past events is inserted into a conversation. But even here the possibilities have not been exhausted. J. B. Priestley's plays (*Time and the Conways* presents this principle in its bare form. It is in a more concealed form in *Dangerous Corner*) are structured so that the events seem to take place before the audience's eyes, but in essence, an action from long ago unfolds, winding a complex tangle of inter-relations.[24] If this is possible in theatre, then it is also available to cinema. As always, our own everyday practice is the school of experience from which a definite principle of composition is drawn.

Montage again provides examples analogous to general composition. In the past, we have discussed how it is possible to shoot a scene of a man entering a room in various ways, depending on the man's mood. Depending on his mood, the room can be shown as large or small. A totally absent-minded man will see incidental things in an arbitrary order. A man preoccupied by thought will see nothing in the room and will bump into furniture. If he has come to look for something, his attention will be directed towards where he can find the object he needs. In all of this, there is already an indication of how to shoot and edit the episode.

As in dramaturgical construction, different principles can be selected in the choice of shooting angles. One can shoot from the character's point of view. For instance, if a man descends a staircase and looks below, the next shot is usually taken looking down from above. At one time, it was believed that the camera's point of view must always be motivated by the character's behaviour. And in 1924 in *The Strike*, when I began shooting a whole series of things from a certain angle, not motivated by a character's vision, this seemed a revolution in camera use and prompted heated debate. Our motto was that you should shoot from the point of view that most fully reveals *your* attitude to the presented material (for instance, if you need to show the correlation of forces in a group scene, you shoot the ground from above, showing the distribution of the forces). This would be the author's point of view—not an indifferent, cold, dry documentary, but an involved point of view with the ability to involve the audience also.

It is important to understand that a gradual, 'non-chronological' unfolding of the theme and comparison of different characters' points of view have the purpose of changing the reader's (or viewer's) point of view on the event, to influence him in the way you would need.

Now, we are ready to analyse a few novellas.

They are interesting in that they refute the idea that the short story is incapable of an absorbing structure or unexpected developments.

Here is a short story by Robert Louis Stevenson called *The Citizen and the Traveller*:[25]

'Look 'round you,' said the citizen. 'This is the largest market in the world.'

'Oh, surely not,' said the traveller.

'Well, perhaps not the largest,' said the citizen, 'but much the best.'

'You are certainly wrong there,' said the traveller. 'I can tell you . . .'

They buried the stranger at dusk.

This short story contains everything needed: characters with personalities (the sceptic traveller and the local man, enthusiastic about his bazaar) and a dramatic denouement. You could not think of a shorter subject.

Here is an even harsher story by Ambrose Bierce, 'The Sheep and the Shepherd':[26]

A Sheep making a long journey found the heat of her fleece insupportable, and seeing a flock of others in a fold, evidently in expectation, leaped in and joined them in the hope of being shorn. Perceiving the Shepherd approaching, and the other sheep huddling into a remote corner of the fold, she shouldered her way forward and said:

'Your flock is insubordinate; it is fortunate that I came along to set them an example of docility. Seeing me operated on, they will be encouraged to offer themselves.'

'Thank you,' said the Shepherd, 'but I never will kill more than one at a time. Mutton does not keep well in warm weather.'

A very short ironic story, with an extremely frightening plot . . . The personality of the sheep is so precisely delineated, it could be acted. Especially, her feeling of superiority over her comrades in the pen, the way she pushes her way to the front, the way she conducts herself in front of the shepherd and the frightening retribution that befalls her.

Now, I will read you Bierce's short story, 'The Affair at Coulter's Notch'.

Ambrose Bierce was a very interesting American writer of short stories who also worked as a journalist. He was a correspondent during the war between the North and South, and his impressions of war are reflected in many of his stories, including this one.

It is important that you understand that Bierce viewed this war in a totally different way from the way that we do. He saw the American Civil War as fratricide, pointless and immoral, which would lead to the degradation and destruction of the nation. For this reason, he usually highlighted the horror and cruelty of war. Bierce's method is very simple—on the one hand, he compresses the horror (his descriptions of war were probably more terrifying than any that had previously been written) and on the other, he debunks certain literary traditions—the extolling of military characters, heroic young women, and notorious front line camaraderie.

I do not think it is necessary to point out that what interests us here is not Bierce's own tendency, but his ability to register this tendency in an engrossing work. Because our immediate task is to express in a representative and absorbing manner *our* ideas and *our* attitude to the war we are in.

And so now, Ambrose Bierce's 'The Affair at Coulter's Notch'.[27]

'Do you think, Colonel, that your brave Coulter would like to put one of his guns in here?' the general asked. He was apparently not altogether serious; it certainly did not seem a place where any artillerist, however brave, would like to put a gun. The colonel thought that possibly his division commander meant good-humouredly to intimate that in a recent conversation between them Captain Coulter's courage had been too highly extolled.

'General,' he replied warmly, 'Coulter would like to put a gun anywhere within reach of those people,' with a motion of his hand in the direction of the enemy.

'It is the only place,' said the general. He was serious, then.

The place was a depression, a notch in the sharp crest of a hill. It was a pass, and through it ran a turnpike, which reaching this highest point in its course by a sinuous ascent through a thick forest made a similar, though less steep, descent towards the enemy. For a mile to the left and a mile to the right, the ridge, though occupied by Federal infantry lying close behind the sharp crest and appearing as if held in place by atmospheric pressure, was inaccessible to artillery. There was no place but the bottom of the notch, and that was nearly wide enough for the roadbed. From the Confederate side, this point was commanded by two batteries posted on a slightly lower elevation beyond a creek, and a half-mile away. All the guns but one were masked by the trees of an orchard; that one—it seemed a bit of impudence—was on an open lawn directly in front of a rather grandiose building, the planter's dwelling. The gun was safe enough in its exposure—but only because the Federal infantry had been forbidden to fire. Coulter's Notch—it came to be called so—was not, that pleasant summer afternoon, a place where one would 'like to put a gun'.

Three or four dead horses lay sprawled on the road, three or four dead men in a trim row at one side of it, and a little back, down the hill. All but one were cavalrymen belonging to the Federal advance. One was a quartermaster. The general commanding the division and the colonel commanding the brigade, with their staffs and escorts, had ridden into the notch to have a look at the enemy's guns—which had straightaway obscured themselves in towering clouds of smoke. It was hardly profitable to be curious about guns which had the trick of the cuttlefish, and the season of observation had been brief. At its conclusion—a short remove backward from where it began—occurred the conversation already partly reported. 'It is the only place,' the general repeated thoughtfully, 'to get at them.'

The colonel looked at him gravely. 'There is room for only one gun, General—one against twelve.'

'That is true—for only one at a time,' said the commander with something like, yet not altogether like, a smile. 'But then, your brave Coulter—a whole battery in himself.'

The tone of irony was now unmistakable. It angered the colonel, but he did not know what to say. The spirit of military subordination is not favourable to retort, nor even to depreciation.

At this moment, a young officer of artillery came riding slowly up the road attended by his bugler. It was Captain Coulter. He could not have been more than twenty-three years of age. He was of medium height, but very slender and lithe, and sat on his horse with something of the air of a civilian. His face was of a type singularly unlike the men about him; thin, high-nosed, grey-eyed, with a slight blond moustache, and long, rather straggling hair of the same colour. There was an apparent negligence in his attire. His cap was worn with the visor a trifle askew; his coat was buttoned only at the sword-belt, showing a considerable expanse of white shirt, tolerably clean for that stage of the campaign. But the negligence was all in his dress and bearing; in his face was a look of intense interest in his surroundings. His gray eyes, which seemed occasionally to strike right and left across the landscape, like searchlights were for the most part fixed upon the sky beyond the Notch;

until he should arrive at the summit of the road there was nothing else in that direction to see. As he came opposite his division and brigade commanders at the roadside he saluted mechanically and was about to pass on. The colonel signed to him to halt.

'Captain Coulter,' he said, 'the enemy has twelve pieces over there on the next ridge. If I rightly understand the general, he directs that you bring up a gun and engage them.'

There was a blank silence; the general looked stolidly at a distant regiment swarming slowly up the hill through rough undergrowth, like a torn and draggled cloud of blue smoke; the captain appeared not to have observed him. Presently, the captain spoke, slowly and with apparent effort:

'On the next ridge, did you say, sir? Are the guns near the house?'

'Ah, you have been over this road before. Directly at the house.'

'And it is—necessary—to engage them? The order is imperative?

His voice was husky and broken. He was visibly paler. The colonel was astonished and mortified. He stole a glance at the commander. In that set, immobile face was no sign; it was as hard as bronze. A moment later, the general rode away, followed by his staff and escort. The colonel, humiliated and indignant, was about to order Captain Coulter in arrest, when the latter spoke a few words in a low tone to his bugler, saluted, and rode straight forward into the Notch, where, presently at the summit of the road, his field glass at his eyes, he showed against the sky, he and his horse, sharply defined and statuesque. The bugler had dashed down the speed and disappeared behind a wood. Presently, his bugle was heard singing in the cedars, and in an incredibly short time, a single gun with its caisson, each drawn by six horses and manned by its full complement of gunners, came bounding and banging up the grade in a storm of dust, unlimbered under cover, and was run forward by hand to the fatal crest among the dead horses. A gesture of the captain's arm, some strangely agile movements of the men in loading, and almost before the troops along the way had ceased to hear the rattle of the wheels, a great white cloud sprang forward down the slopes, and with a deafening report the affair at Coulter's Notch had begun.

It is not intended to relate in detail the progress and incidents of that ghastly contest—a contest without vicissitudes, its alternations only different degrees of despair. Almost at the instant when Captain Coulter's gun blew its challenging cloud twelve, answering clouds rolled upward from among the trees about the plantation house, a deep multiple report roaring back like a broken echo, and thenceforth, to the end of the Federal cannoneers, fought their hopeless battle in an atmosphere of living iron whose thoughts were lightnings and whose deeds were death.

Unwilling to see the efforts which he could not aid and the slaughter which he could not stay, the colonel ascended the ridge at a point a quarter of a mile to the left, whence the Notch, itself invisible, but pushing up successive masses of smoke, seemed the crater of a volcano in thundering eruption. With his glass he watched the enemy's guns, noting as he could the effects of Coulter's fire—if Coulter still lived to direct it. He saw that the Federal gunners, ignoring those of the enemy's pieces whose positions could be determined by their smoke only, gave their whole attention to the one that maintained its place in the open—the lawn in front of the house. Over and about that hardy piece the shells exploded at intervals of a few seconds. Some exploded in the house, as could be seen by thin ascensions of smoke from the breached roof. Figures of prostrate men and horses were plainly visible.

'If our fellows are doing so good work with a single gun,' said the colonel to an aide who happened to be nearest, 'they must be suffering like the devil from twelve. Go down and present the commander of that piece with my congratulations on the accuracy of his fire.'

Turning to his adjutant-general he said, 'did you observe Coulter's damned reluctance to obey orders?'

'Yes, sir, I did.'

'Well, say nothing about it, please. I don't think the general will care to make any accusations. He will probably have enough to do in explaining his own connection with this uncommon way of amusing the rearguard of a retreating enemy.'

A young officer approached from below, climbing breathless up the acclivity. Almost before he had saluted, he gasped out:

'Colonel, I am directed by Colonel Harmon to say that the enemy's guns are within easy reach of our rifles, and most of them visible from several points along the ridge.'

The brigade commander looked at him without a trace of interest in his expression. 'I know it,' he said quietly.

The young adjutant was visibly embarrassed. 'Colonel Harmon would like permission to silence those guns,' he stammered.

'So should I,' the colonel said in the same tone. 'Present my compliments to Colonel Harmon and say to him that the general's orders for the infantry not to fire are still in force.'

The adjutant saluted and retired. The colonel ground his heel into the earth and turned to look again the enemy's guns.

'Colonel,' said the adjutant-general, 'I don't know that I ought to say anything, but there is something wrong in all this. Do you happen to know that Captain Coulter is from the South?'

'No; *was* he, indeed?'

'I heard that last summer the division which the general then commanded was in the vicinity of Coulter's home—camped there for weeks, and—'

'Listen!' said the colonel, interrupting with an upward gesture. 'Do you hear *that*?'

'That' was the silence of the Federal gun. The staff, the orderlies, the lines of infantry behind the crest—all had heard, and were looking curiously in the direction of the crater, whence no smoke now ascended except desultory cloudlets from the enemy's shells. Then came the blare of a bugle, a faint rattle of wheels; a minute later, the sharp reports recommenced with double activity. The demolished gun had been replaced with a sound one.

'Yes,' said the adjutant-general, resuming his narrative, 'the general made the acquaintance of Coulter's family. There was trouble—I don't know the exact nature of it—something about Coulter's wife. She is a red-hot Secessionist, as they all are, except Coulter himself, but she is a good wife and a high-bred lady. There was a complaint to army headquarters. The general was transferred to this division. It is odd that Coulter's battery should afterwards have been assigned to it.'

The colonel had risen from the rock upon which they had been sitting. His eyes were blazing with a generous indignation.

'See here, Morrison,' said he, looking his gossiping staff officer straight in the face, 'did you get that story from a gentleman or a liar?'

'I don't want to say how I got it, Colonel, unless it is necessary'—he was blushing a trifle—'but I'll stake my life upon its truth in the main.'

The colonel turned towards a small knot of officers some distance away. 'Lieutenant Williams!' he shouted.

One of the officers detached himself from the group and coming forward saluted, saying: 'Pardon me, Colonel, I thought you had been informed. Williams is dead down there by the gun. What can I do, sir?'

Lieutenant Williams was the aide who had had the pleasure of conveying to the officer in charge of the gun his brigade commander's congratulations.

'Go,' said the colonel, 'and direct the withdrawal of that gun instantly. No—I'll go myself.'

He strode down the declivity towards the rear of the Notch at a break-neck pace, over rocks and through brambles, followed by his little retinue in tumultuous disorder. At the foot of the declivity, they mounted their waiting animals and took to the road at a lively trot, round a bend and into the Notch. The spectacle which they encountered there was appalling.

Within that defile, barely broad enough for a single gun, were piled the wrecks of no fewer than four. They had noted the silencing of only the last one disabled—there had been a lack of men to replace it quickly with another. The debris lay on both sides of the road; the man had managed to keep an open way between, through which the fifth piece was now firing. The men?—they looked like demons of the pit. All were hatless, all stripped to the waist, their reeking skins black with blotches of powder and spattered with gouts of blood. They worked like madmen, with rammer and cartridge, lever and lanyard. They set their swollen shoulders and bleeding hands against the wheels at each recoil and heaved the heavy gun back to its place. There were no commands; in that awful environment of whooping shot, exploding shells, shrieking fragments of iron, and flying splinters of wood, none could have been heard. Officers, if officers there were, were indistinguishable; all worked together—each while he lasted—governed by the eye. When the gun was sponged, it was loaded; when loaded, aimed and fired. The colonel observed something new to his military experience—something horrible and unnatural: the gun was bleeding at the mouth! In temporary default of water, the man sponging had dipped his sponge into a pool of comrade's blood. In all this work there was no clashing; the duty of the instant was obvious. When one fell, another, looking a trifle cleaner, seemed to rise from the earth in the dead man's tracks, to fall in his turn.

With the ruined guns lay the ruined men— alongside the wreckage, under it and atop of it; and back down the road—a ghastly procession!— crept on hands and knees such of the wounded as were able to move. The colonel—he had compassionately sent his cavalcade to the right about— had to ride over those who were entirely dead in order not to crush those who were partly alive. Into that hell he tranquilly held his way, rode up alongside the gun and, in the obscurity of the last discharge, tapped upon the cheek the man holding the rammer—who straightaway fell, thinking himself killed. A fiend seven times damned sprang out of the smoke to take his place, but paused and gazed up at the mounted officer with an unearthly regard, his teeth flashing between his black lips, his eyes, fierce and expanded, burning like coals beneath his bloody brow. The colonel made an authoritative gesture and pointed to the rear. The fiend bowed as a token of obedience. It was Captain Coulter.

Simultaneously, with the colonel's arresting sign, silence fell upon the whole field of action. The procession of missiles no longer streamed into that defile of death, for the enemy also had ceased firing. His army had been gone for hours, and the commander of his rearguard, who had held his position perilously long in the hope of silencing the Federal fire, at that strange moment, had silenced his own. 'I was not aware of the breadth of my authority,' said the colonel to anybody, riding forward to the crest to see what had really happened.

An hour later, his brigade was in bivouac on the enemy's ground, and its idlers were examining, with something of awe, as the faithful inspect a saint's relics, a score of straddling dead horses and three disabled guns, all spiked. The fallen men had been carried away; their torn and broken bodies would have given too great satisfaction.

Naturally, the colonel established himself and his military family in the plantation house. It was somewhat shattered, but it was better than the open air. The furniture was greatly deranged and broken. Walls and ceilings were knocked away here and there, and a lingering odour of powder smoke was everywhere. The beds, the closets of women's clothing, the cupboards were not greatly damaged. The new tenants for a night made themselves comfortable, and the virtual effacement of Coulter's battery supplied them with an interesting topic.

During supper, an orderly of the escort showed himself into the dining room and asked permission to speak to the colonel.

'What is it, Barbour?' said that officer pleasantly, having overheard the request.

'Colonel, there is something wrong in the cellar; I don't know what—somebody there. I was down there rummaging about.'

'I will go down and see,' said a staff officer, rising.

'So will I,' the colonel said; 'let the others remain. Lead on, orderly.'

They took a candle from the table and descended the cellar stairs, the orderly in visible trepidation. The candle made but a feeble light, but presently, as they advanced, its narrow circle of illumination revealed a human figure seated on the ground against the black stone wall which they were skirting, its knees elevated, its head bowed sharply forward. The face, which should have been seen in profile, was invisible, for the man was bent so far forward that his long hair concealed it; and, strange to relate, the beard, of a much darker hue, fell in a great tangled mass and lay along the ground at his side. They involuntarily paused; then the colonel, taking the candle from the orderly's shaking hand, approached the man and attentively considered him. The long dark beard was the hair of a woman—dead. The dead woman clasped in her arms a dead babe. Both were clasped in the arms of the man, pressed against his breast, against his lips. There was blood in the hair of the woman; there was blood in the hair of the man. A yard away, near an irregular depression in the beaten earth which formed the cellar's floor—a fresh excavation with a convex bit of iron, having jagged edges, visible in one of the sides—lay an infant's foot. The colonel held the light as high as he could. The floor of the room above was broken through, the splinters pointing at all angles downward. 'This casemate is not bomb-proof,' said the colonel gravely. It did not occur to him that his summing up of the matter had any levity in it.

They stood about the group awhile in silence; the staff officer was thinking of his unfinished supper, the orderly of what might possibly be in one of the casks on the other side of the cellar. Suddenly the man whom they had thought dead raised his head and gazed tranquilly into their faces. His complexion was coal black; the cheeks were apparently tattooed in irregular sinuous lines from the eyes downward. The lips, too, were white, like those of a stage negro. There was blood upon his forehead.

The staff officer drew back a pace, the orderly two paces.

'What are you doing here, my man?' said the colonel, unmoved.

'This house belongs to me, sir,' was the reply, civilly delivered.

'To you? Ah, I see. And these?'

'My wife and child. I am Captain Coulter.'

This story's plot can be told in a few words: a general forces his personal enemy, a captain, to fire upon his own home with his wife and child inside. Strategically, this attack is utterly pointless. Thus, taking advantage of the circumstances, the general avenges himself on the captain.

But how adroitly Bierce threads this plot!

An untalented person would structure something quite different from this material. He would exploit the idea of the general avenging himself by forcing the captain to fire upon his own family. His choice of a title would already give the plot away. What would be the name of a film like this? *The General's Revenge*!

First, he would provide an exposition of the war using archival footage. Then he would demonstrate Coulter's bravery: 'CAPTAIN COULTER WAS VERY BRAVE.' Coulter beating Southerners seven times (in seven shots). Fade-out.

ONE DAY A NORTHERN REGIMENT STOPPED AT COULTER'S HOME

Captain Coulter's home. The Captain's wife greets them cheerfully. The General likes her. They settle in. Dinner. The General praises Coulter's bravery (shown in the exposition, now repeated in words). An incident with the wife (depending on the director's taste). Discipline prevents

Coulter from demanding satisfaction. Coulter is a very strong-willed man. Fade-out.

SEVERAL MONTHS LATER. Southern regiments in action (also archival footage).

COULTER'S HOUSE IS CAPTURED BY SOUTHERNERS. Coulter's house is attacked. The Southerners enter. The wife does not greet them cheerfully. The wife and child are arrested and locked up in the cellar (they are shoved in by the soldiers' rifle butts).

The scenes with the General. He recognizes Coulter's house in the distance. Recalls the incident. (This memory is probably conveyed by some song, like 'This street, this house . . .')[28]

A fiendish plan: the General forces Coulter himself to fire upon this house. The struggle between love and duty is shown on Coulter's face for a long time. The sense of duty wins out, followed by the deafening blast of the first exploding shell.

A long battle. Its first phase: fire and counterfire (again intercut with archival material, even though the difference of quality is obvious). The crossfire ceases; as a tribute to cinema,[29] shots of the Southerners elegantly dying in Coulter's house.

Coulter's wife and child, trembling in the cellar. Blood seeps into the ground of the cellar.

Coulter shoots. The shell hits the house, killing the wife and child. The raid on Coulter's house (a half-hour of non-archival material).

The Captain races to the cellar. The bodies of his wife and child (naturally, this shot will be taken from the one where they are killed because, as usual, they will have forgotten to take a separate shot of the bodies). Coulter in despair over the bodies. The General leaves with a devilish smirk. Fade-out.

That would be a typical, talents treatment of a subject, which step by step illustrates 'the General's revenge'. The chronology of action demonstrates 'how everything happened'. Everything is clear: the General is a scoundrel, Coulter is a brave man, and his wife is a sacrifice. And there are no shocks to be had.

A resolution would usually be put on the script of such a film: 'There's something here.' Indeed, there is something here: a man fires upon his own house, but the subject is developed straightforwardly and very superficially. Therefore, a second phrase is likely to appear in the resolution: 'Tighten it up!' The script will return to the studio with the conclusion: 'For this production, a strong actress is needed to flesh out the role of the wife.' Take note: the role of the wife is not vivid enough and therefore, 'a strong actress is needed.' But if you remember, the role of the wife in Bierce's story is that of a corpse!

Bierce's narrative is extremely clever.

Coulter's bravery is made known in the very first conversation, but how? Through the General's doubt, which is clouded by the Colonel's unswaying confidence. But we ourselves are soon forced to suspect that the Captain is not brave.

The conversation between the General and Colonel is cut short by the instructions which so disturb Coulter. The description of 'Coulter's Notch' begins the line of battle episodes; each successive episode will repeat the theme of this description (the threat to Coulter's life) with greater intensity.

After resuming the first conversation in which the General's doubt turns into open sarcasm, Bierce describes Coulter's arrival and every detail in this description interests us. We have barely formed an impression of the Captain's selfless courage when we see him disturbed by his orders to fire upon the house. The reader naturally assumes that his uneasiness derives from a fear of danger; after all, there is not even the slightest hint of any other explanation.

Coulter hesitates, almost refuses, but no—he agrees. Structured on the principle of the triple blow.

At the same time, the motif of the house is planted somewhere in the subconscious. This is preparation for a line which has not yet been made explicit.

In the battle descriptions, there is a constant hint of the possibility of Coulter being killed. The phrase 'If he's still alive' is casually thrown out. This is done in order to emphasize the danger of Coulter's position, but also to introduce the idea that the General intends ultimately to kill him.

The conversation between the Colonel and the Officer. The Colonel is proud of the artillerists' heroism, but still calls the attack senseless ('It's odd. What could he have been thinking of?'). This is the first hint that something might be wrong. The motif of the senselessness of the General's order is emphasized by the fact that the enemies' cannons could be knocked out by rifle fire. The comment 'something is wrong' is made in conversation.

So Bierce prepares us in three directions:

1) by demonstrating the senselessness of the order;

2) by casting doubt (what was the General thinking of?);

3) by hinting that something is wrong.

Later, we learn that Coulter owns a plantation and that the General once set up camp there. Soon it will become clear that it is this very plantation being fired upon and that at some time the General had had a falling-out with Coulter. At that moment an interruption occurs: 'Listen!' (not to a sound which breaks the silence, but to the silence that falls over the cannons. Remember how, in *The Grapes of Wrath*, the people were awakened when the noise of the hurricane stopped?).[30] The knocked-out cannon is replaced by a new one, only then is the interrupted conversation resumed.

There is now no doubt that the General sent Coulter there so that he would be killed. With deep indignation, the Colonel orders the firing stopped—perhaps too late. The situation is further aggravated by the fact that Lieutenant Williams has been killed, which means Coulter might also be dead. The Colonel and his scouts rush to the 'notch'. The descriptions emphasize the horror, the feeling of hell.

But the General's revenge did not succeed—Coulter is alive. Since the text does not end here, we expect there to be an epilogue, most likely a confrontation between Coulter and the General.

Although the house was bombarded with fire, it still stands. But in this apparent calm, the motif of something being wrong arises again. The descent into the cellar. A false conclusion: the hair of the dead woman is mistaken for a beard. Then there is a digression—the conversation about the casemate. And only in the final words is the outcome made known—one phrase reveals the General's revenge.

I want to point out that this is not a trick ending such as O. Henry uses. Henry employs the trick ending mechanically. It is unexpected for the first two or three stories, but after that you are unable to mathematically deduce a reverse structure. In more complex and refined subjects, the reverse structure is unexpected and sharp; it arises, not mechanically, but from within the inner contradictions of the events. Think of Shakespeare's endings (in *Romeo and Juliet*, for example).

Getting back to Bierce, it is necessary to point out that so far we have touched on only the outstanding compositional structure of the story. And it certainly is engrossing and interesting from the viewpoint of narrative construction. But besides this, notice how masterfully and keenly Bierce's own attitudes are revealed throughout the entire plot development.

By showing the horrors of war, Bierce debunks the idea of friendship between Generals and subordinates, which the sugar-coated literature of America had traditionally fostered. He demonstrates that the same kind of 'friendship' that Northerners and Southerners had for each other could also exist between a General and Captain within the Northern army. But Coulter, a Southerner by birth, is on friendly terms with the Colonel. Thus, Bierce suggests that there can be friendship between Northerners and Southerners under normal conditions.

The situation by itself does not reveal the author's attitudes; that is obvious. A situation similar to the one told here by Bierce could also take place in the present war—it is possible that a man could be forced to fire upon his own house. The treatment of the situation depends on the author; is it the base upon which he constructs human interactions which contain his personal opinions of these characters.

If you should have to shoot a war scene in which people fire upon their own home, you will need to find the human reactions that would be characteristic and typical of us, and be able to reveal the conflicting passions present in such a situation.

The most important thing is to pay attention to human interaction. The weakest aspect of our short fictional films is the virtual absence of uniqueness in the characters and their interaction. It is always patriots that are shown. Always fine Commanders. Always fine mechanics. But nuances and differences between people and their feelings are important. For, each person loves his homeland *in his own way*.

2

I am now going to read you two scripts which are based on an identical situation. It is developed superficially in the first case, but in a complex and meaningful way in the second.

First, we shall examine Nikolai Shpikovsky's script, 'The Banner',[31] which contains a fine dramatic knot—an old woman poisons some Fascists who have captured her town. And lest they suspect the food she gives them is poisoned, she herself eats some of the poisoned food and dies with them.

Leonid Leonov took this script for the basis of his own and reworked it. I think that Leonov's version is an outstanding example of masterful, cinematic narrative.

I will read you [Shpikovsky's] 'The Banner'.

A group of partisans approach a forest.

Middle-aged farmers, old men, woman, children. Fighting youths—girls and boys.

Women on horseback. Men walking along-side them, leading cattle. And, even though these are simple families fleeing their village captured by the Fascists, the detachment has the look of true partisans.

Most are armed. Rifles and two machine guns are loaded on one of the horses.

Those who have no weapons arm themselves best as they can.

At the last moment, before continuing into the woods, they pause and look below at the village they have left. It is spread across the valley. All around, the fields are ablaze and smoke rises towards the sky. The village itself has become a smoking furnace.

The scorched skeletons of huts and deserted streets are all that meet the enemy when it enters the village.

The iron plate bearing the name of the collective farm is charred, but the words 'Free Ukraine' stand out distinctly, as though cleansed by the flames.

One of the Fascists, who apparently knows Ukrainian, reads the name of the collective farm in his thick Galician accent,[32] swears, and tears the sign down with the end of his bayonet.

But even here in the rain and dust, it continues to live; shafts of sunlight dance joyfully upon the brilliant cleansed metal plate and the words 'Free Ukraine' stand out brighter and larger than before.

Grey-green uniforms can be seen throughout the village.

They burst into the huts still standing from the flames.

But everything is empty. Only a few people have stayed behind—old men and women who could not leave.

They rummage through everything, breaking and destroying [things] with the wild brutality of barbarians. They smash whatever comes to reach—babies' cribs in abandoned nurseries, radio receivers left in club rooms, light bulbs hanging in peasant huts.

They ransack chests. They make off with any remaining belongings. They burst into huts. Screams are heard, crying, women wailing.

Then gunfire—and everything is quiet.

Then another hut is broken into—and the same thing is repeated.

A frail old man is dragged out into the street.

'You won't talk?'

The old man is silent.

Again: 'Speak up or you'll be sorry.'

The old man is silent, still.

Then the one who screamed at the old man (whom we recognize as the Galician who tore down the plaque) draws out his revolver and fires at point-blank range.

The old man falls before he even has a chance to scream. The murderers pay no attention and continue on.

Old Granny Odarka stands before an icon with a burning lamp, crossing herself, whispering her prayers.

Shooting and screaming is heard from the streets.

The glow of a fire is visible in the window.

Odarka is sixty-five, but still in good shape. Time has treated her in a unique and special way. She is grey, stooped over and covered with wrinkles, but something youthful, energetic and lively has kept her from becoming truly old.

Odarka is dressed in her best clothes, as though for a holiday—the way women dress in Ukraine for saints' days or special occasions.

When the Fascists burst into her hut, Odarka does not even turn round.

So engrossed is she in prayer, it would seem that she has not heard what has taken place in her village: the burning, the screaming, the wailing, the shooting.

She does not hurry to respond to the shouts of those who have burst into her hut. She finishes her prayer first, stands up, crosses herself, and only then turns to face them.

The icon, the lamp, the old woman praying—all this makes an impression upon the Galician. He makes a signal to the others and goes up to the old woman.

'Praying to God? That's good.'

The old woman looks at him severely and says in a stern voice:

'You take your headgear off. You're standing before an icon, you heathen.'

'What do you mean, heathen? I believe in God,' he says, taking off his helmet.

'Cross yourself!' the old woman demands sternly.

The Galician crosses himself.

Then the trusting old woman becomes friendly and kind.

'These days I divide people up according to God,' she explains. 'Those who believe in God and those who don't. Those without God are without salvation.'

With a prophetic gesture she points to the window in which the blazing fire is reflected.

'There is no salvation. A circle of fire. Holy bread perishes in flame. Everyone's gone. But where can you hide from God? Nowhere!'

More Germans come into the hut. Now there are fifteen of them.

'Do your people believe in God?' she suddenly asks, glancing at the group of Germans. 'Maybe they're heathens, like my old man?'

'And where is your old man?'

'Gone. Left with the rest of 'em.'

'And why didn't you leave?'

'Why should I? They don't believe in God. They've forgotten God, and He's forgotten them.'

The Germans say something to the Galician. He explains. They are relieved.

The Galician turns to the old woman.

'Got anything to eat, Granny?'

'Of course. For good people who believe in God, I always have something.'

And, continuing to mutter prayers and fuss, the old woman starts to set the table. She brings out bread, two pitchers of milk, some butter, and honey. She does it all with expert and agile movements.

'They went into the woods?' asks the Galician, translating for one of the Germans.

'What do you mean, the woods? When the army retreated, they left with them,' explains the talkative old woman. 'Thieves hide in the woods, but our people are peaceful. They fled from fear. But what's there to be afraid of? Without God, even your hair's not safe on your head.'

The food is now laid out on the table. Before they begin, the Germans ask the old woman to try it herself. Not understanding why at first, she modestly refuses.

Honoré Daumier, 'Freedom of the Press—Do Not Touch it!': 'you have the impression that the figure moved, jerked from phase to phase'.

Tintoretto, 'Ariadne, Bacchus and Venus': 'flying figures . . . literally
depicted as a spiral'.

TOP: Michelangelo, 'Morning' from the Tomb of Lorenzo de' Medici: 'a feeling of tragic constraint (movement which strains, but cannot break loose) finds a plastic embodiment'.

FACING PAGE: Michelangelo, Tomb of Lorenzo de' Medici, Florence: 'each element of the body in the two reclining figures is in a different position of movement'.

FACING PAGE & TOP:
Michelangelo, two different views of 'Twilight' from the Tomb of Lorenzo
de' Medici: 'the joints of the bodies are in different stages of movement',
but he 'tries to bind movement'.

'Go ahead and eat, for Heaven's sake! I'll eat something.'

'But maybe it's, maybe you ... We don't know you.'

Only then does the old woman guess why they will not eat.

'It's a sin to think that,' she says. 'it's you who are trained to kill people. People are the same as animals to you. I've lived a long life, thank the dear Lord for it. It's been good and bad, but to commit such a sin!'

She drinks the first glass of milk and eats some bread.

After that, the others begin eating.

A young boy of twelve runs through the woods, exhausting himself, barely able to move his legs. His shirt is in rags. His feet are bare.

He fights his way through the thicket, shoving branches aside. Here and there, he crawls, then jumps back on his feet.

Evening. It is already dark in the forest.

Having posted guards, the partisans settle themselves in the deep gully.

Mothers feed their children.

They cannot light a fire: water, bread and butter is all they can eat.

The sounds of the forest. Silence.

A guard suddenly hears something.

'Who's there?'

The young boy crawls out from a bush at the guard's feet and answers:

'It's me, Uncle Vasili.'

He tries to stand up but is too weak.

The guard pulls him up. The boy is surrounded by partisans. Excited and out of breath, he sobs for a few minutes and then speaks.

'They killed everyone. Uncle Nikanor, Aunt Masha. As soon as they enter a house, they shoot them. They questioned others, asked where you went. Anyutka too. She started to scream, and they took their rifles and . . .' The boy can no longer control himself and starts to howl.

'Don't cry now, Andreika,' they comfort him. 'Are there many of them in the village, the Germans?'

'They all left,' sobs Andrei. The only ones left are in Old Odarka's house.'

'They didn't kill her?'

'Why should they? She laid the table for them. They're all sitting and eating. Even the one that killed my sister Anyutka,' and again Andrei starts to cry.

The partisans whisper among themselves.

A group of twenty break off. They gather their rifles and one of their machine guns.

They try to turn one of the girls back, but she insists and joins the unit.

Checking their weapons, one after the other disappears into the thicket.

In Old Odarka's house, the dinner has come to its end. Almost everything has been eaten.

'Eat,' Odarka urges them. 'Nobody makes honey like our collective farm.'

The old woman clears off the table and glances at the grandfather clock. More than an hour has passed since they began eating.

Walking around her guests, she studies their faces carefully.

'Well, did you like my food? No one leaves Old Odarka's place hungry.'

She continues to fret and fuss over them: 'I always manage to find enough for everyone. To feed them or however God wills they be rewarded for their deeds.'

Again, she looks at the clock and then carefully around at the faces of her guests.

I'm a sorceress,' she tells the Galician. 'I know every herb, which ones are healthy or cure diseases, which ones you can die from.'

Continuing to clear off the table, the old woman speaks calmly, as though talking about the most trivial matter.

'I picked one of those herbs once. I thought to myself, why should I? One should save peoples' lives; death will come anyhow. But I picked it all the same, just in case. Suddenly you meet such people'—the old woman's voice becomes stern and loud.

Everyone automatically turns towards her.

'People who can't even be called people. They say they believe in God and they hack innocent children to pieces and shoot old men.'

'What's up with you?' the Galician jumps to his feet.

But Old Odarka cannot be stopped.

'I thought I'd have no use for deadly herbs. But there I needed one,' she points to one of the Germans who clutches at his chest, and with a distorted face, falls from his chair.

A second starts to breathe irregularly.

The Galician jumps up and draws out his revolver. But he also is too weak to raise his hand.

'You can go ahead and shoot now. It doesn't matter, we're both going to die.' It is already difficult for the old woman to talk; she cannot breathe. 'How much evil you monsters have already committed . . . I stayed behind . . . on purpose . . . fixed for you . . . you devils . . . something to eat . . .'

One of the Germans draws out his revolver. Takes aim.

But at that moment, a shot rings out.

The German falls from the bullet.

Rifles are pointing through all the windows.

But, by the time the partisans run into the house, there is no one to shoot at. Most lie writhing on the floor, and those still on their feet can offer no resistance.

They rush to the old woman. She lies on the floor with closed eyes. They raise her up and sprinkle water on her face.

She opens her eyes for a moment and recognizes the faces of friends and family.

And, looking from one to the other, she says goodbye to each person separately.

'Goodbye, Vasili. Goodbye, Nikita. Goodbye, Mikola. Goodbye, Fedor. God grant you all live to be old. But, if you have to die, then take your own life. The way. Old Odarka . . . took hers.'

She closes her eyes, but finds the strength to raise herself and whisper to the girl partisan, who bends over her, supporting the old woman:

'And you, Marusya. Don't surrender to anyone. Our banner, which you won in my brigade.'

The old woman is silent.

They bury her that night in the forest near the gully.

The lake shines silver under the moon. The forest is silent.

And, when she is lowered into the ground, Marusya steps forward and unfolds what she has held so carefully in her hands.

And when it unfolds, everyone sees that it is a red banner.

The girl kneels down and drapes the banner into the grave, covering Old Odarka with it.

'Comrades,' she says with a tearful voice, trembling from emotion. 'We now say goodbye to our dear Old Odarka for the last time.'

Marusya stops. Everyone is quiet. The forest rustles.

Overcoming her emotions, Marusya finishes her short speech.

'We have won this banner. It has passed from one to another, selecting those who best serve our Motherland. We place it now in this grave with Old Odarka because she won it at the cost of her life; it must be passed no further.'

Odarka's husband also steps forward, a tall and stern old man.

He stands by the grave with his rifle in his hands.

'Goodbye, old dear,' he says warmly to his wife, as though she were still alive.

He returns to the group. He looks at them all, the stern, resolved faces, their determined gaze, the men and woman with rifles in hand, thinks to himself and says:

'I look at all of you, my comrades, and I'm happy. I'm happy that no one is crying at this bitter moment, because we must not cry now. Tears wash away man's bitterness and hatred, but we must keep them alive inside us, so that they won't give us a day's or night's peace, not until the last German dog is driven from our precious Motherland.'

He falls silent and gazes ahead into the dark forest, as though seeing there the future he describes:

'The years will by go. Grass will grow again. A fresh wind will blow over a new Soviet harvest. Our grandchildren will gather together in the "Free Ukraine" collective farm to cry. They will remember our Old Odarka with fine words, and recall her heroic life and death.'

A typical script, isn't it?

The author's intention is superb. His material is drawn from documents, but his inability to develop the situation greatly weakens the script.

Now we shall examine the second version of the script, written by Leonid Leonov.

A sky with billowy, peaceful clouds. Suddenly there is a whistle, and the sound of shrapnel from the middle of a forest. Cut to a title:

The Feast at Zhirmunka

The sound of incomprehensible clanging and voices, the murmur of excited voices. But the eye sees meadows and copses in the calm summer stillness. Then we look down and see: something is going on in a sprawling, border village. Endless rows of peasant houses surrounded by greenness. In front of the village Soviet, weapons are being handed out to the inhabitants. It is a very businesslike and impressive sight. A truck with weapons, the driver playing with the motor. At the same time, a man whose head is bandaged with a torn shirt distributes weapons from above. The line at the truck is short; the distribution is almost over. There are young people there, but most are elderly. The first, for various reasons, were turned down for army conscription, among them a teacher with thick glasses which greatly magnify his eyes. But there are many perfectly healthy young men among them who are not old enough. The elderly, having received their weapons, test the bolt, look down the barrel—experience from previous wars.

The man distributing the weapons hands them out quickly, fitting each weapon to its recipient. Thus, the teacher receives a Berdan rifle with a well-worn hand-strap. The lad of sixteen is given a sabre with a tattered sheath. And old man Oneisim gets a bear-hunting musket with two boxes of cartridges tied to it so they will not be lost. The old man looks something like a bear: bearded, with deep-set eyes; this man speaks only when he has something to say, and then tersely, without conversation. Stuffing the cartridges into his pockets, the old man holds his hand out for more, but there are no more.

'What a beauty! To give out something like this and it doesn't even waste gun powder.' He is pleased with his sturdy and solid weapon.

'Come on, step lively now!' cries the dispenser, meeting the next man's gaze. 'And don't crowd around, men. You're at war now.'

And again, the doleful, unfriendly whistle.

'Spread out,' Oneisim says calmly.

The men take cover; several press up against the truck. Old Oneisim, the man in the truck and the driver stay put. The first from pride, the other two for lack of a place to hide. Exploding shrapnel. A starling flies off its perch. Clouds of dust rise up from the hail of bullets in the road. A chicken with its tail shot off spins around in the deserted road, drawing circles in the dust with her wing.

There is the difference between these two scripts. Lifelike characters on the very first page, each one sharply delineated. They are shown already in action. Their personalities are marked, details are found—the startled starling, the shot chicken—which prepare you for Fascist brutality.

Oneisim glances with amusement at the chicken, then in the direction of the shot.

'Missed. Huh! Some prize shooting. Just you wait, we'll give you a prize you won't be able to carry away with both hands!'

He walks through the village, nodding with respect to those he passes. Everyone is hurrying. He passes the kindergarten. A sign on the outside reads, 'THE RED ZHIRMUNKA COLLECTIVE FARM PIONEER CLUB'. Children peer out through the window. They all know Oneisim and call out to him:

'Grandfather! Grandfather!'

'Oneisim Petrov has a weapon!'

'Grandfather Oneisim, show us how a bear walks around a beehive. Show us!' says the youngest.

Oneisim looks at them for a moment. There is great kindness and concern in his deep-set eyes. And suddenly, he decides. Even though he is in a hurry, he performs his famous routine, beating off swarms of stinging bees. The children howl with laughter. The kindergarten teacher comes out on to the porch, and the children hush. They do not really understand what is going on. And besides, children are always curious at grown-ups' business. They try to listen.

'That's very nice, Oneisim Petrovich.' Then she turns to the window and says sternly, 'Get away from that window, children. How many times do I have to repeat myself?'

'March away from the window, like you were told!' orders Oneisim.

'Better take the kids to the woods before long,' Oneisim says quietly without looking at the teacher.

'We've taken most of them there, Oneisim Petrovich. Only a few of the older ones are left. A cart's on its way now for them and our things.' Then with a sigh, she says: 'What's going to happen, Oneisim Petrovich? They're like beasts, attacked all at once. I heard . . . you're leaving Zhirmunka?'

He does not answer right away, and rests the heavy musket on his shoulder.

'We'll pick them off from the woods. When they start to yawn, we'll send a bird right into their mouth. They'll screw up their eyes and we'll let 'em have it. It's too late now. An eye for an eye!'

He tilts his cap and walks off. More shrapnel, only louder. The bullets fall upon the ground and moss-covered roofs. The ricochet of lead breaks the silence.

Oneisim enters a peasant house with his musket in hand.

The long, dark hallway is filled with neatly arranged mats and shelves; bunches of herbs and rhizomes are strung along the walls. Here Oneisim comes across a young girl holding her child and his wife—a tall, portly woman with a stern, well-preserved face. She is holding a bag containing some kind of potion.

Coming through the door, Oneisim says, 'are you at it again, Paraska? I should let you both have it. I told you not to, you stubborn old woman!'

'Don't be angry, Oneisim Petrovich,' begs the young mother with the child. 'Where could I find a doctor today? My child couldn't sleep all night. Just cried and cried. Look at him, Oneisim Petrovich—he's covered with spots all over.'

See how the herbs are worked in here?

Praskovya (Oneisim's wife) says softly:

'Good. Be sure to boil this herb into a thick brew, add an egg and some honey. Let it cool off, and the rub it on him here, that's right, onto his chest while you pray. And that'll do it.'

The interior of the peasant house. A frightening and solemn word has broken the peaceful quiet—war. The table is set with a brass samovar resting on a brick, large round meat pies, a honeycomb in a hand-painted wooden dish, and empty cups. Between them stands a glass with a silver holder at the head of the table. There is no one sitting at the table. Oneisim's son is sitting on a bench in the corner, changing his shoes. Like his mother, he has light brown hair and is thin, but he has his father's piercing and deep-set eyes. He slowly and carefully wraps his feet with clean cloth in the fashion of a peasant, so they will not be rubbed raw during the long walk. His wife is also wearing boots and a hunter's belt with ammunition fastened tightly around her waist; she is energetic and has thin, lively eyebrows. Preparing to leave with the men, she packs a loaf of bread and a cloth in her bag tightly, so as to fit in as much as she can. The arms they have already been given stand in the corner by the stove, not far from the oven forks.

'All right, c'mon, c'mon . . . let's get a move on!' says Oneisim. He picks up the belt from the bench and fastens it tightly outside his short quilt jacket. 'They've already whistled from the pasture.'

'Already, General?' asks the young girl, not without malice, flashing her row of fine teeth. 'Always orders.'

'He is a General'—laughs the son, reaching for his other boot. 'A General has to be frightening. So that the enemy will fall from a single glance of his, eh General?'

Oneisim says, 'He won't fall from a glance. We'll have to give him some help falling down.'

Quiet preparations. The bag is packed, the boots tied. The young girl takes a sip of tea, but does not swallow it. The mother comes in.

'Say goodbye to your mother, you brat,' says Oneisim to his son, who takes something out of his pack.

The son goes up to his mother. She makes the sign of the cross over him.

'Beat them, my son. Let them have it right in their filthy black jaws. Beat them till your last breath. Goodbye. Perhaps we'll see each other in spring.'

Oneisim says softly, 'Take off your cap when your mother blesses you.'

Piotr takes his cap off and lowers his eyes.

'You don't want to come with us, Mother?' he barely asks. 'You could be in charge of the house-keeping in our dug-out.'

'Where could I go, son? My home is here. I danced here when I was a young girl. My father died here. I raised you on that bench there and threw your wedding party here, too. How can I leave here? It's not stolen, but was earned by sweat.'

Oneisim: 'I've already tried, but she doesn't want to.'

Praskovya: 'There's only one dug-out waiting for me. And that one I'm not afraid of.'

Shrapnel explodes right outside the window. She listens: 'Listen. Practically fell in the well.'

Oneisim: 'They're scratching the sky, the villains! And the sky will scratch them back. Well, let's have a seat before leaving.'[33]

They all sit down according to custom and then rise again. A knock at the window; time to leave.

The four of them leave the house.

A slanted back porch. Intricately carved railings. Oneisim mechanically peels off a thin strip of chipped paint and crushes it between his fingers. Pensively:

'Always meant to re-do this porch. My nephew promised to send us some whitewash, but I guess he forgot . . . OK, afterwards!'

'Time to move on, General,' says Pyotr. He sees a young boy running directly towards them along the garden path.

'Don't worry, Mother. Grinka here will stay with you.'

The boy runs up, out of breath.

'Oh! What a battle's going on over there! Trucks are pouring out of the gully!'

Pyotr: 'We heard it, we heard it, son. You help your Grandmother if she needs anything. Go on in the house now and sit on the stove. They won't shoot at the stove.'

He looks at his father and is embarrassed that his father shakes his hand as a man. Says goodbye to his mother. She does not cry, but screws up her eyes and practically bares her teeth, like a mother-wolf protecting her young. She looks down at him and gently pushes him by the shoulders:

'Go on.' And the boy leaves without looking at her, his head bowed.

We see here an authentic, human attachment for one's home and one's birthplace. This is not the act that the old woman in Shpikovsky's story puts on, but a true attachment to one's home. The motive is changed, but here it is understandable why the old woman stays behind.

The three of them step off the porch. The young couple head off quickly. The old woman closes the door. The sound of it being bolted. The old man stops on the path by the cherry trees whose berries are not yet ripe.

See how the details are done?

    . . . Suddenly he calls out:

    'Paraska!'

    No answer. Then louder and stronger:

    'Come out here, Paraska.'

    Praskovya comes back out on to the porch.

    'I said come over here. Hurry up!'

    Praskovya walks over to him.

    'Well what is it, old man? Forget something?'

    Oneisim is unusually upset. After a pause: 'Listen. Hide my tea holder, or bury it in the ground. These Germans are rotten. It's a bad hour . . .' And again a pause. 'Why were you cooking supper today?'

    'Because I'm making turkey, that's why. If it's tough, you won't touch it with a stick. It has to boil all day.'

    'Ah! Well, go ahead, boil it, boil it,' and he smacks his lips. Another pause. Suddenly, he looks up from the ground. 'Well, let me say goodbye to you too, Paraska!'

Silence. She hugs him around the neck and rests her head on his shoulder. No one sees them. He says softly:

'I've never hurt you, have I?'

'Never, old man.'

'And I tried to convince you, right, Parasya?'

'You've tried, old man. It's OK. We've had a good life, old man . . .'

Silence, and then suddenly Oneisim straightens up. He says in the tone of a sharp command: 'All right, all right. What're you drenching my shoulder for? All right! You're making an old woman out of me. I order you to go back inside now.'

He turns away and heads for the gate. The old woman picks a wild flower on the path and trudges back to the house.

Isn't that well done? Think about the episode with the flower. The old woman feels young again. All our impressions of her are elevated to a new level. The same thing with Oneisim's position as head of the house when he picks the paint off the railing. And the love scene between the old couple is so well played—she bends down and picks a flower. Well done!

Then a fade, and the sounds of war. The distant rattling of trucks and machine-gun fire. There are no great battles here. The fate of Zhirmunka will not be decided here. Planes pass overhead, like a knife in the heart. The sound of being wounded. And everything becomes quiet. Trucks drive along the empty street—a German motorized infantry. The soldiers look all around; they are uneasy at the deserted village and the lack of resistance. The wheel of a car runs over a chicken just shot. One car stops in the village and the others continue further.

Their teeth shining, the soldiers get out of the truck on command. It is not clear why they are so happy at this moment: perhaps to brace themselves from fear? We see all this from afar. Breaking into small parties, the soldiers spread out to the various houses. Another silence. Somewhere, the sound of glass shattering. Somewhere, the painful screaming of a woman. Somewhere, the cracking of a window shutter being torn away, and suddenly, the piercing squeal of pigs. Followed by an immediate outburst of laughter. The enemy enjoys trampling what someone else has that is good. But an empty street is seen on the screen. A breeze stirs old willows and ripples the water in a pond. We do not witness the horrors—they burst through with sounds. We do not need to see them. But suddenly, for some reason, a grinding bar flies through a glass window, for some reason, a column of smoke begins to spread from under the doors of an old barn.

Four German soldiers come out of one of the houses, very businesslike and satisfied. Two of them are carrying a trunk—the spoils of war? They throw their loot into the truck. Then the foursome heads for the Pioneer Club. They beat on the door with their rifle butts. They wait for it to be opened. They wait and glance at each other. The faces of the frightened children are seen in the covered window and someone's hand pulling them back—a woman in a white smock. Someone cracks the door slightly, a pair of eyes peer out and immediately tries to slam the door, but one of the soldiers places his knees in the crack. Eye to eye. Terrifying. The soldier bares his teeth. It is already too late to close the door. Two of them push the third through the door, joking, as they close it behind him. A woman stands on the other side of the door. A little girl with a raggedy doll stands behind her, holding on to her skirt. The little girl does not cry and even tries to smile. Then the sound of a child's screaming and crying is heard coming from the room. The woman's voice:

'Be quiet, children! Children . . . calm down!'

The soldiers go in, the door is shut behind them. And again, nothing is heard. Again, the empty street. The smoke of a fire starting, a chicken, a pole where the bird house had sat. The wind scatters papers in front of the Village Soviet.

The door of the Pioneer Club is opened. Four soldiers silently come out. Their empty hands hang by their sides. They have become heavy from carrying. For some reason, one of them fetches two rifles from his comrade-in-evil. The soldiers do not look at each other. Neither their eyes nor even their faces can be seen beneath their helmets. They are no longer laughing. When the door is opened, the doll is seen lying on the doorstep, flung aside and trampled by boots. The hall is now empty. And this silence is more terrifying than the fiercest battle.

One of the soldiers issues an abrupt command, pointing to the next house. An order to continue the search? He then utters 'Heil!'—from a desire to instil courage in himself? Cautiously and carefully, he shuts the door behind him, as though afraid of disturbing someone. He tiptoes down the steps. An escape? He then greedily drinks water from the well, like a crane—the well is for watering cattle. He drinks straight from the bucket . . .

See? The brutality of Fascism is shown not through a direct action or deed, but through a detail f the behaviour of a man who 'drinks from a cattle trough'.

The three enter the neighbouring house. The fourth runs to catch up with them.

Again, Praskovya's house. She sits idly and attentive at the table. She stands up and walks over to the stove. The mechanical movements of a person whose daily routine has been disrupted. A sharp knocking from outside. She picks up an axe and goes to open the door, preparing herself. Not them! A woman jumps towards her in the darkness. She does not speak, but moans something in the hall between clenched teeth. She staggers and falls against the wall. Despair. He blouse is in rags and there is a large scratch on her cheek.

'Run! Run! They're on their way here now.'
She lets out a cry and at the same time says softly:
'Even our children.'

Praskovya caresses her head. She is a bit taller
than her pathetic guest. Authoritatively and calmly,
she leads the woman into the house; only her
mouth has become twisted. Now it is clear that
this is the schoolteacher. How changed she has
become in this one hour. And again, on the bench,
she whispers softly and sobs:

'. . . the children.'

'Hush now, hush! I know. You don't have to
say it—I understand. A mother always senses her
son's blood. Hush now, for goodness sake pull
yourself together. Here, drink some.' And reaches
for some water.

The other shakes her head, 'I can't, it'll make
me sick, Parasha. The children . . .' And again,
some incomprehensible movement of her lips.

And again, they sit. Praskovya sits up straight
and rigid.

The little boy peeks from around the stove,
hiding his head. He is curious at this grief which
he does not yet understand. The women are

holding each other's hands. The sounds of foot-steps and the grandfather clock—that is all.

The teacher grows quiet. She starts to droop, but then suddenly jumps up.

'Oh! I still have to run over to Arina's. Her sister-in-law and her two kids are over there.'

Praskovya sees her to the door. Alone now, she thoughtfully rearranges the things on the table left there since the morning. Her face shows no emotion.

'Looks like I've been left alone for this feast today. No one's going to come, neither friend nor foe.' She walks over to the adjacent pantry.

She goes up to a small bin. Above it hang agricultural posters. Something like 'First aid for drowning' and 'What is pyrethrum?' She removes the lid. The simple and pungent pharmacopoeia of the country doctor is stacked in this pantry. She carefully selects various herbs, reaching for the most important one at the very bottom.

An hour passes (all the while, the grandfather clock going 'tick-tock', 'tick-tock') before the soldiers come to Praskovya's house. Her doors are not locked. They cross the hall from the porch, probing the darkness with their bayonets. One of them kicks the door open and jumps to the side. But there are no shots. He goes in. Two others cover him from the rear. Praskovya is praying.

A low-hanging icon case with dark faces, several burning candles, some ribbons and a rolled-up scroll. A soldier steps forward and walks in front of her. He wants to see the old woman's face and what she is up to. Silently, she turns her face to the side, crosses herself again and stands up. She turns around to face the soldiers.

The soldier opens up the icon case and scrutinizes the various objects: no, there's nothing dangerous here.

One of the soldiers goes over to the table. Such great temptation! In addition to what was there before, there is now a turkey with legs sticking up on a painted wooden dish, honeycomb and cheese tarts. Everything that Zhirmunka is famous for! Unable to control himself, the soldier grabs the pitcher of milk. His rifle is propped against the table.

The Sergeant enters the room. He has a wolfish, but not unattractive face, a helmet and an automatic pistol. He sees the soldier with the milk. A quick blow to the pitcher with the handle of his pistol. Fragments and splashes. There is a thick line of milk on the stunned soldier's moustache. He had not had a single drop. Praskovya shakes her head over this scene.

A warning in German about being careful in a foreign country. 'You're not at home, dog!'

A kitten runs up and starts lapping at the white puddle on the floor. He likes it and sticks his tail up. Full, he washes his face with his paw.

Everyone watches the kitten in suspense. Silence. A smile gradually comes over their faces. One of them, evidently grateful for the experiment, squats down to play with the kitten. It paws at the soldier's dangling handkerchief. They all exchange glances with each other. Only the Sergeant's face is stern and set. He picks up a cheese tart, examines it as though it were a museum piece, and carefully puts it back. Could such an appetizing thing as this golden crusted cheese tart really explode? More soldiers are now peering through the window. News of the wonders in this house has already spread throughout the village. The Sergeant calls to one of the soldiers he recognizes standing outside the window. The soldier comes inside. He quickly salutes from the doorway. A whispered conversation about something. 'Yes sir!' in German. The soldier pulls a small, tattered book from his pocket, a phrasebook of ready translated phrases. He speaks to Praskovya.

'What's your name? Anna? Pelagei?'

'What? How can I be a Pelagei? I'm a woman. Praskovya is my name.'

'Come here, Praskovi.'[34]

He places her before him as though she were a wooden object.

'Do you believe in God, Praskovi?'

'Huh! Young man, God is our protector. You young people may not believe, but I'm old. But I advise you, young man, not to forget God.'

It is obvious that the soldier does not understand everything, but all the same, he says:

'Uh-huh.'

He translates for the Sergeant. An exchange of opinions. All agree.

'The Russian God commanded for men to feed the hungry and give drink to the . . . the th-th-thirsty. Do you know that, Praskovi?'

'What's that? Give drink to whom, young man?' asks the old woman, moving slightly closer.

'The th-th-thirsty,' the improvising translator pronounces with difficulty.

She understands and smiles.

'Who doesn't know that? Our parents instilled the word of God in us. We carry it in us to the grave. Eat if you're hungry. Our house is full, don't be shy. Everything is already made.'

A pause.

'Why is that table already set?'

'I was expecting guests, young man. But then all this commotion started. You need the table to spread your plans out on? It'll just take a second to clear everything off.'

And she starts to take away the boiled turkey.

'That's not necessary,' says the Sergeant himself in Russian. And suddenly, 'You eat it yourself.'

'I'm already full, Commander. Don't worry about me. You don't starve to death standing over the stove.'

The Sergeant looks at the kitten playing.

'No. Eat that.'

He says it as a command and points at the food.

'Well, I'll sit with you and keep you company. I'll drink some tea.'

She smiles at their distrust. In the peasant fashion, she takes a bite of cheese tart and then leisurely sips her tea, blowing at the steam on top. It appears to be tasty and delicious. And everyone stares entranced, frozen, like spectators at some magnificent performance, at her hands, at the movements of her lips. They hand her things, as though waiting on her, she refuses nothing.

'Thank you, sonny. They didn't tell us you're all so polite.'

Her grandson, who earlier had peeked nervously from behind the stove, now moves over to the bench and watches in horror at Praskovya enjoying herself.

One of them can no longer control himself. Sniffing one of the cheese tarts, he places it between his anticipating lips. A second and third hand reaches over his shoulder. Several sit down at the table.

'Eat, eat! We obey any authority. We treat others as they treat us. Eat up, children.'

By now the entire house is filled with soldiers. They stuff themselves. No, this is unlike any other feast Zhirmunka has ever seen. The collective farm's abundance has proved useful. One of the soldiers, fatter than the others, loosens his belt wider. And then we see that the kitten is on his knees. It purrs when the back of its ears are scratched. On the table now there is also a bottle of home-brewed beer which is fast being emptied. It is the kind of bottle usually used for transporting acid.

The German soldiers begin singing. Discordant male voices. The old woman walks off and comes back with delicious homemade blood sausage. Her every step is followed by a soldier. One of them clasps her shoulder and starts to hug her. She slaps his hand.

'I've been a married woman for thirty-eight years now, you silly German.'

She walks away again, this time alone. She motions her grandson to get down off the bench. He understands. The singing becomes louder, monotone and unpleasant to the ear. The little boy quietly slips off the bench. They do not see him.

They are absorbed in their singing. One soldier conducts the others: their faces are strained.

Praskovya goes out on to the porch and sits down. The smile disappears from her lips. She breathes heavily. She hears the singing from inside. The look of death is in her eyes. Her outspread hand falls heavily against the floorboard.

Again the interior of the house. Everyone is singing. Drunken, concentrated faces. Zeal.

The Sergeant is silent. The soldier with the kitten on his knees scratches it mechanically. He looks down: surprise. Its head thrown back, the soft kitten lies motionless on his uniform trousers. The soldier cries out wildly (in the middle of the singing), and with superstitious terror, knocks the kitten off on to the floor. He falls back against the wall. There is great confusion. Everyone jumps up. And again, though already doomed, they look at the tiny grey animal: it lies motionless, its little paw barely twitching. Perhaps it is even trying to crawl away. Silence. And in the silence the grand-father clock ticks. By now they all realize what has happened, and no one wants to believe it. Only one soldier continues to stuff himself, having found some more food on the windowsill in the pantry. He does not know yet. He comes out content, chewing.

'Halt!' cries the Sergeant as loud as he can. His voice is racked with spasms. He jerks the tablecloth off and on to the floor.

Everyone snaps to attention. He looks at their faces one by one. Is it true? Their faces are already somehow changed. One sits down suddenly on the bench and undoes his collar. He can no longer stand up. Another loses his sense of recognition and gazes aimlessly around the house. A third starts to cry. Someone runs to the well to drink and falls down on the ground. The feast is over in Zhirmunka.

The little boy crawls out from behind the stove. The Sergeant shoots at him, practically at point-blank range. He misses. Fragments of broken pottery from the shelves, plaster from the stove. So many people, and they cannot get the child. Several do not even make an attempt to catch him.

Praskovya is sitting on the porch. Her hair is practically soaked and has fallen over her forehead. Leaning her back against one of the porch columns, she looks at the crushed wild flower in front of her (the one from saying goodbye to Oneisim).

The little boy bends over her, 'Grandma, you want some water? I'll get some, grandma?' And again, 'Grandma, why did you eat with them?'

Through her teeth, and sternly, she says 'Run, tell 'em. Grandma has 'em on a leash. Only tell 'em to hurry. Maybe they have something. Run!'

'Grandma!'

'Run! Since I was twelve I've carried the whole load. Now it's up to you, Grinka. Run.' The boy runs off.

The boy runs out of the village. He crawls in the burdocks so as not to be noticed by the guard posted at the edge of the village. Bushes. He is not shown, only the branches of a hazelnut tree moving. Circles on the surface of the water—crossing the stream. Twigs crack—running. Two shots above his head and again silence. A bird whistles. A guard on the bridge raises his rifle but is unable to fix his target and lowers his weapon. One partisan is hardly worth making a scene over.

The porch. Praskovya finds the strength to stand up and go into the house. I think every step she takes should be shown. The calm face has become pinched and a terrifying look has come over her features. She goes inside and looks around. The kitten is on the floor. Two soldiers sit on the stove with their legs sticking out; another lies on the bench. Not one has stayed in his previous position.

The Sergeant is at the table. Runny cheese drips from an overturned dish on to the floor, forming a small puddle. The white liquid drips on to his knee. His pistol, no longer needed, has been thrown into the puddle.

The old woman looks at this fallen army:

'Why don't you eat, you brave young men? Or have you had your fill of Russian bread, my uninvited guests?'

The Sergeant is still alive. His veins are protruding and he is rigid. With great effort, he drags the pistol over to him. But his fingers lack the strength to cock it, in spite of the enormous efforts he makes to do so. Sweat on his brow.

Praskovya goes inside the pantry. Her Susanin mission has come to its end.[35]

A little later, the partisans re-enter the village. Oneisim fires a well-aimed shot from his musket at the guard. Crossfire. By evening, the partisans reach Praskovya's house.

The deadly scene of the feast in Zhirmunka. The first to enter is Petrov's young wife. Others follow her. Silence. Then she catches sight of Praskovya in the pantry—she is sprawled out, motionless, on her bed, her arms hanging over the sides. The young bride's eyes become fierce and piercing. She comes out and walks past the dead bodies. It is clear who was the leader here. She walks up to the Sergeant and slaps him in the face with the back of her hand.

'You monster, take what you have coming to you, you bastard!' and she strikes him again.

The body rolls but does not fall, pinned against the wall.

And then, Oneisim's voice is heard from the pantry, 'Quiet out there, no noise! There's a lioness lying in here. A dead lioness who defended her home to the end!'

Well, what do you think? Is it well written?

Who can explain what makes it good? What is the difference between these two versions?

It's always unpleasant to pull to pieces a fine work of art, but we need to understand the virtues of Leonov's script. Only don't say things like 'the dialogue is good'. If you like the dialogue, try to explain what makes it good—the richness of language, an unexpected phrase, or an uncompleted thought prompted by something unimportant. Since we've talked so much about straightforward plot developments, it'll be interesting to analyse how Leonov avoids them.

Tell me what your impressions are.

VOICE FROM THE ROOM: Leonov handled the departure of the partisans and the formation of their detachment very well. The handing out of the weapons introduces us to the inhabitants of the village, each of whom is characterized by some feature. This is not the formless, faceless mass of the first version of the script, but life-like people we will remember and from whom we can judge what life has been like in Zhirmunka till now.

Leonov sets up the Germans' poisoning very well, through the old woman's sorcery. Her sorcery is not constantly presented, only the fact that she makes medicine with herbs, and at first the herbs lead us up a blind alley. We don't suspect that she has stayed behind to take revenge. The realization that the old woman might have done something occurs when her grandson watches in horror as the old woman eats. And later he says, 'Why did you eat?', meaning he had seen her preparing it. But, in Shpikovsky's version, it's not clear where the little boy comes from; he simply witnessed the old woman eating.

Leonov's dialogue between the old couple is very good.

EISENSTEIN: In what way is it good?

FROM THE ROOM: Their conversation reveals the tragedy of people forced to leave their homes. And this conversation also reveals the relationship between the old couple.

EISENSTEIN: In this conversation, there is again an accumulation of untrue associations. They talk about the tea holder, but this is really just a pretext for the old man because he does not want to talk about what is most important. Like the herbs, this detail is wonderfully selected by the author. It conceals the true thematic line at work here, and at the same time, serves to illustrate the character's personality. The old man's feeling of responsibility for the household is shown, but it is not at all a matter of an ascetic, overwhelming feeling for what he owns, for a silver tea holder that he doesn't want to lose. Leonov depicts man realistically, as opposed to the works of certain other authors where characters have absolutely no feeling of attachment to their property. Of course, in some cases, the need to destroy one's property could be felt stronger than an attachment to it, but there are no saints who wouldn't feel this sense of attachment. And this doesn't have anything to do with ideological matters; we are simply saying that the collective farmer lives well. And how precisely Leonov presents the second detail: the old man is sad that he has to leave before he could taste the turkey that he wouldn't touch with a stick.

FROM THE ROOM: The conversation about the turkey points to the meal the Germans eat. The turkey is played up to the end.

I also like the way Leonov presents the Germans' arrival very sparingly, in as few details as possible.

AGAIN FROM THE ROOM: When you compare the two versions of the script, you can't help but notice that Shpikovsky piles on the horrors of war, and that Leonov does not show them. I've seen Pudovkin's footage; he shows the papers lying in front of the Village Soviet and an empty street. This has a much stronger effect than showing Germans bursting in with rifle butts.

EISENSTEIN: It's another illustration of the use of understatement as the strongest and most effective device.

By refraining from showing the Fascists' violence in the kindergarten, you feel the full weight of the tragedy.

FROM THE ROOM: It's good that Leonov has the Germans come to the old woman's house after they have committed their horrible deeds in the village.

EISENSTEIN: That's an extremely important moment in the film. The spectators' feeling of hatred for the occupiers must be built to such a degree, that the retaliation against their actions is felt as completely natural. The structure of the script has the old woman going through the bin for herbs after the arrival of the kindergarten teacher, so that the act of poisoning is perceived as a direct response to this tragic visit (even though in all likelihood, the old woman had made this decision long before this moment).

FROM THE ROOM: But before this, she is walking around with the axe. This axe deflects any suspicions that the old woman will poison the Germans.

EISENSTEIN: That's right, it gives the impression that she will use the axe on the Germans.

FROM THE ROOM: In order to force the old woman to eat first, the Germans will have to talk to her. In Shpikovsky's version, the German who knows Russian is simply ludicrous, but in Leonov's version the very witty conversation takes place with the aid of the phrasebook. It's also good that the German waits on the old woman.

EISENSTEIN: Again, he plays with a false development. She is a smart old woman and understands very well what they want. But she pretends it is politeness, good treatment of the populace.

FROM THE ROOM: In the first version, the old woman's speech about the poisoning is very crude.

EISENSTEIN: Once the Moscow Art Theatre staged something by Chekhov, which contained a long monologue that didn't work very well.[36] Chekhov had already left for the Crimea and promised to send them a rewrite. A telegram was received from him a few days later: 'A wife is a wife'—in place of the entire long monologue.

Leonov tries to find just the right word, a unique nuance of personality. In connection with this, I will read you some words by Flaubert, which Maupassant included in his introduction to *Pierre and Jean*:

Talent is long patience.

Everything you want to express must be considered so long, and so attentively, as to enable you to find some aspect of it which no one has yet seen and expressed. There is an unexplored side to everything, because we are wont never to use our eyes but with the memory of what others before us have thought of the things we see. The smallest thing has something unknown in it; we must find it. To describe a blazing fire, a tree in a plain, we must stand face to face with that fire or that tree, till to us they are wholly unlike any other fire or tree. Thus, we may become original.

Then, having established the truth that there are not in the whole world two grains of sand, two flies, two hands, or two noses absolutely alike, he would make me describe in a few sentences some person or object, in such a way as to define it exactly, and distinguish it from every other of the same race or species.

Whatever the thing we wish to say, there is but one word to express it, but one verb to give it movement, but one adjective to qualify it. We must seek till we find this noun, this verb, and this adjective, and never be content with getting very near it, never allow ourselves to play tricks, even happy ones, or have recourse to sleights of language to avoid a difficulty.[37]

With Shpikovsky, everything is approximate and undefined—some old man, some woman, some partisans. Remember, how in the beginning of his script some old man appears, God knows where from, who must say God knows what. And it doesn't even say why the Germans are killing him. Or the Germans smash to pieces the cribs just because there are cribs in the village. And how crudely the relay banner is brought in which 'must be transferred no further'. And it is to accompany the old woman to the grave. That's the same kind of view of Soviet reality that superficial foreigners have who write: 'The Soviet people spend their time handing a banner to each other, which is why they call it a relay banner'. The title of his novella makes this banner the central motif (and what a *flimsy* title for a film—'The Banner').

But Leonov's title right away presents a striking development of his theme—'The Feast at Zhirmunka'. A peasant table set with simple food is called a 'feast'. This has associations with (Pushkin's) 'Feast in the Plague Year' and 'Belshazzar's Feast'—the thing is instantly elevated to tragic proportions.[38] This gives the director a precise indication of the degree of intensity with which he needs to express the theme of the script. And it is no accident that Leonov writes in the end of his novella: 'the Susanin mission'. It is very important that the *Susanin* motif is perceived as central.

These words, 'the Susanin mission', provide a tonality to the development of the images of the old man and woman. 'Praskovia' must be elevated to a large collective image which embodies the heroism of man—Susanin. But they also contain a precise approach for the director—how the novella should be shot, a precise stylistic key. For instance, poisoning with herbs could be associated with unpleasant physiological reactions (they cause sickness, weakness, the Germans' staggering, etc.). Clearly, the scene should be raised above this sort of specific, realistic reaction to [be given] a universal meaning.

Of course, it would be a mistake to shoot *The Feast at Zhirmunka* in the manner of Dovzhenko's *Shchors* or *The Earth*, which lie beyond everyday reality.[39] If the old man's speech about 'the lioness' is elevated to [the level of] an almost monumental generalization, then the conversation about the tea holder is conducted on a somewhat different level. Here, the statuesque quality of Dovzhenko would give it far too great a tragic quality.

I think Leonov's novella should be realized in the manner of the first scenes in Pudovkin's *The Mother*, where the director achieved a quality of true tragedy without breaking with the realistic 'letter'. Compared to Gorky's novel, Pudovkin went a little further in his stylistic generalization, something which cannot be said of the film, *The*

Artamanov Affair, which falls way short of the expressiveness of Gorky's sketch.[40]

Gorky had a stylistic key—his relation to factories: 'I'm afraid of factories; they're like wild beasts.' One must be able to feel and formulate things like this.

In addition to descriptions of things like actions and characters, a true writer's works always contain a fully defined stylistic 'order': shoot it this way—this way and no other. In such cases, the style of the film, the manner of shooting, even the arrangement of individual shots must be realized in the key of the writer or author of the script.

Here is your assignment for our next class.

We liked two details which very strongly revealed the personalities of the main characters. I'll read them to you again—'Oneisim mechanically peels off a thin strip of chipped paint and crushes it between his fingers. Pensively, "Always meant to re-do this porch. My nephew promised to send us some whitewash, but I guess he forgot. OK, afterwards!"' And also: 'The old woman picks a wild flower on the path and trudges back to the house.' I ask you to think of how you would direct and shoot these two scenes (their length, shooting angle, etc.), taking into account the psychological weighting of these details and their significance in the general development of the action. Because these are not incidental, but are the key scenes with which you should begin your shot breakdowns. You should also try to imagine how the old man should be standing over the body of the old woman when he says 'lioness', how the door is closed in the kindergarten, how the German would stick his knee in the cracked door, and how near and from which side it should be shot.

Don't concern yourself with complex stylistic questions, don't struggle with graphic problems of the shots— do it so that the meaning of the inner-shot action is clear. A shot should be like a line in a poem—self contained, and its idea must be absolutely crystal clear.

NOTES

1 A transcript of lectures given by E to his class on direction at VGIK [the All-Union State Institute of Cinematography] on 11 and 18 September 1941, following the Nazi invasion of the USSR on 22 June. E's lecture addresses the problems facing film-makers in directing the 'Fighting Film Albums' [*boevye kinosborniki*], which each consisted of a series of short film stories and which constituted a key element in the cinema's fight to maintain Soviet wartime morale. In a sense they were the World War II successor to the *agitki* of the Soviet Civil War period.

2 The so-called 'Leninist proportion' was never in fact defined by Lenin but was derived from his Directive on Cinema Affairs of 17 January 1922, which stated that 'for every film programme a definite proportion should be determined' between entertainment and propaganda films, the latter made in the format soon to be itself defined as 'documentary'. See: *FF*, p. 56.

3 Directed by Vsevolod I. Pudovkin (1893–1953) and Mikhail I. Doller (1889–1952), *Feast at Zhirmunka* [*Pir v Zhirmunke*] was incorporated into the sixth fighting

film album of 1941. The role of Odarka was played by Anastasia P. Zuyeva (1896-1986).

4 Leonid M. Leonov (1899-1994), Russian prose writer and playwright, probably best know for his novels *The Badgers* [1924] and *The Thief* [1928].

5 *ESW3*, pp. 16–41; cf. 'Film Form: New Problems' in *FiFo*, pp. 122–49.

6 During the Cultural Revolution of 1928-32 and subsequently montage cinema was viewed with increasing suspicion by the political leadership of the industry, headed by Boris Z. Shumiatsky (1898–1938), who favoured the creation of 'living' characters with whom the audience could more readily identify in his pursuit of a cinema that was 'intelligible to the millions'.

7 Fyodor M. Dostoyevsky (1821–81), one of the leading Russian novelists of the 19th century.

8 Maurice Leblanc (1864–1941) was the French author of numerous stories involving Arsène Lupin, master of disguise, gentleman thief turned detective who more than once outwitted Sherlock Holmes and almost always the police. The first Lupin story appeared in 1905 and many film versions were made of Leblanc's subsequent tales.

9 Novel in verse form by the leading Russian writer, Alexander S. Pushkin (1799–1837).

10 Alan Upchurch has used: Pyotr Ilyich Tchaikovsky, *Eugene Onegin*, trans. Vladimir Nabokov (New York: Pantheon Books, 1964), VOL. 1, p. 105.

11 Eduard K. Tisse (1897–1961) was E's cameraman from *The Strike* right through to *Ivan the Terrible*,

although for this last film he was responsible only for the exteriors.

12 A reference to the discussions at the January 1935 conference of Soviet film-makers. E's contributions to the conference are in: *ESW3*, pp. 16-46, and other speeches are translated in: *FF*, pp. 348-55.

13 Ben Jonson (1573–1637), English poet and dramatist. *Volpone* [1605] was one of his major plays.

14 Lev N. Tolstoy (1828–1910) was the other towering novelist of 19th century Russia.

15 Lion Feuchtwanger (1884–1958), German Jewish writer who emigrated to the USA, first published his play *Jew Süss* in 1918. It was made into a film, known in the USA as *Power*, by Lothar Mendes in 1934, starring Conrad, Veidt and misappropriated as the basis for the eponymous anti-Semitic Nazi propaganda film directed by Veit Harlan in 1940.

16 The heroine of Tolstoy's *Resurrection*.

17 Honoré Daumier (1808–79) was a French painter, graphic artist and caricaturist who specialized in caricatures of the contemporary middle classes and their pretensions.

18 Jacopo Robusti, known as Tintoretto (1519–94), Venetian religious painter.

19 Michelangelo Buonarotti (1475–1564), Italian painter, sculptor and poet. The Medici family tomb is in a funerary chapel attached to the church of San Lorenzo in Florence. The two figures referred to here are those of Giuliano and Lorenzo de' Medici, symbolizing the Active and the Contemplative Life. Beneath

them are the four equally famous symbols of Time and Mortality—*Day* and *Night* (again representing the Active Life) and *Dawn* and *Evening* (standing for the Contemplative Life).

20 Reference to the fictional characters in the series of stories by Sir Arthur Conan Doyle (1859–1930).

21 Edgar Lee Masters (1868–1950) published this anthology in 1915.

22 Joseph Conrad (1857–1924) was a British novelist, born in Ukraine of Polish parentage.

Ford Madox Ford (born Hermann Hueffer Ford, 1873–1939) was the grandson of the Pre-Raphaelite painter Ford Madox Brown (hence the change of names) and collaborated with Conrad on various works, including the novels, *The Inheritors* [1901] and *Romance* [1903].

23 Ernst Theodor Amadeus Hoffmann (1766–1822) was one of the leading writers of German Romanticism. The full title of this work is: *The Life and Opinions of the Tomcat Murr: Together with a Fragmentary Biography of Kapellmeister Johannes Kreisler on Random Sheets of Waste Paper*, ed. E. T. A. Hoffmann (London: Penguin, 1999).

24 John Boynton Priestley (1894–1984) was a British novelist, playwright, critic and broadcaster. His plays, *Dangerous* Corner [1932] and *Time and the Conways* [1937] form part of the 'Time' plays, so called because of the use they made of the theories expounded in J. W. Dunne's *An Experiment with Time* [1927].

25 The text used here appears as Fable XII in: *Robert Louis Stevenson: Collected Works*, VOL. 20, *Letters and*

Miscellanies (New York: Charles Scribner's Sons, 1898), p. 475.

26 The text used here comes from: *The Collected Works of Ambrose Bierce* (New York: Gordian Press, 1966), p. 331.

27 This story appears in Vol. 2 of *The Collected Works of Ambrose Bierce.*

28 A popular song used in the Kozintsev & Trauberg film *The Youth of Maxim* [Iunost' Maksima, 1934].

29 Presumably a reference to *Birth of a Nation* [USA, 1915], directed by D. W. Griffith.

30 John Steinbeck (1902–68), American novelist, published *The Grapes of Wrath*, a sympathetic and realistic portrayal of the plight of migrant agricultural workers in California, in 1939. It was immediately made into a film directed by John Ford, starring Henry Fonda, and released in January 1940.

31 Nikolai G. Shpikovsky (1897–1977), Soviet scriptwriter and journalist, whose story 'The Banner' [Znamia] was adapted by Leonid Leonov for the screen as *The Feast at Zhirmunka.*

32 The Western part of Ukraine formed part of Polish Galicia between the First and Second World Wars. It still has the reputation of being the part of Ukraine where nationalism has been most strongly felt.

33 The reference is to the Russian custom of sitting for a moment in silence before someone leaves on a journey.

34 The gender confusion in the Russian here makes the German soldier a figure of mockery. The Russian speaker would know that most women's names end in '-a' and that a name ending in '-i' (such as Praskovi or Pelagei, mentioned earlier) could not belong to a woman.

35 Ivan Susanin was a peasant folk-hero who misled the enemy army during a 17th-century invasion. He is best remembered as the central character in the opera *A Life for the Tsar* [1835] by Mikhail I. Glinka (1804–57).

36 Anton P. Chekhov (1860–1904), Russian dramatist whose later years were closely associated with the Moscow Art Theatre.

Guy de Maupassant (1850–93) was a French novelist and short-story writer of the Realist school.

37 Alan Upchurch here used: Guy de Maupassant, *Pierre and Jean,* trans. Ernest Boyd (New York: Alfred A. Knopf, 1925), pp. 16–17. The novel was first published in 1888.

38 Pushkin's 'little tragedy' [*malen'kaia tragediia*] *Feast in the Plague Year* [Pir vo vremia chumy], was written in 1830 and published in 1832. It is based on the verse volume *The City of the Plague* [1816] by the critic John Wilson (1785-1854), which re-created the atmosphere of London during the Great Plague of 1665.

In the Bible (Daniel, ch. 5) Belshazzar was the son of Nebuchadnezzar and King of Babylon in the sixth century BC. At a lavish feast he used the vessels taken from the Temple in Jerusalem: a mysterious hand warned him that in so doing he was committing a sin and later that night he was assassinated.

39 *The Earth* [Zemlia,1930] and *Shchors* [1939] were made by the Ukrainian director Alexander P. Dovzhenko (1894–1956).

40 *The Artamanov Affair* [Delo Artamanovykh, 1941] was directed by Grigori L. Roshal (1899–1983).